LEADERSHIP JUST
GOT PERSONAL

LEADERSHIP JUST GOT PERSONAL

STORIES & THOUGHTS ABOUT LIFE & LEADERSHIP

STEVEN FULMER

Steven Fulmer, Inc.
PO Box 91284
Portland, OR 97291

www.FulmerSpeaks.com
Printed in the United States of America
First Steven Fulmer, Inc. publishing edition March 2012

Graphic design by Brian Lockyear
Cover design by Julia Fulmer
Cover Photograph by Kimber Dahlquist

ISBN 978-0-9850073-0-0

For Julia, Sarah and Leah

"If your actions inspire others* to dream more, learn more, do more and become more, you are a leader."

— John Quincy Adams

*The "others" you inspire may just well include yourself!

Contents

PREFACE

I'm proud of this book, not because I have any sort of illusion that it's an international best-seller, or the best book ever written. That's not the source of my pride. I'm proud simply because it is done! In this simple act of completion I demonstrate one of the greatest and most simple truths about leadership.

Jim Collins said it brilliantly: "*Good is the enemy of Great*," and in the context in which he stated it, I would agree. However, it is equally accurate in other circumstances to say, "Great is the enemy of Done!" This book isn't about it being great; it's about it being done.

What did Woody Allen say? *"80% of success is just showing up!"* Sometimes leadership is about inspiring ourselves and others, and sometimes leadership is simply about showing up. Sometimes leadership is the simple ability to keep moving forward at whatever level of perfection, or dare I say, imperfection, one can muster. Greatness will come, not in one fell swoop, but gradually. Suddenly one day, you will wake up and realize you have been the leader you sought to be all along.

Leadership isn't about always being the best or perfect; someone will always be better. Nor is it about having all the answers, because some days you don't. Leadership is about having the courage and tenacity to keep going when you are scared and beaten down by the internal forces of self-doubt and unworthiness or the external forces of opposition and criticism. "I'm not good enough" or "I'm not ready" are the paralyzing mantras that have destroyed more leaders than any other force. Leadership is often about the determination to say "yes," when "no" would be easier or less embarrassing. Or saying "no" because "yes" would mean not having to disappoint anyone even though the "yes" would take you off track or lead you astray from your vision.

Leadership is hard, but not for the reasons most people seem think. It's hard because whether we are leading ourselves or others, leadership demands the ability to believe that we have value and worth *both* as individuals and as measured against others. It's not about being better or worse than others, but simply knowing that we are worthy to lead just as we are and for the unique gifts we bring to the table.

Many of us fail to step into our leadership because we fail to acknowledge that worthiness. In our heads we hear stories about our lives and too many of us listen only to the ones telling us that we are not good enough, smart enough, strong enough, tall enough, pretty enough. Why? And compared to what? No matter what measurement we pick someone will beat us, until we realize that our leadership isn't a function of others, it's a measurement of self, the ability most days to simply beat our own personal best rather than besting some-one else's.

As a first book, this completed product you hold in your hands, is most definitely a beating of *my* personal best, not because it's better than any other book you will ever read, but because it is better than any other book I have ever written.

ACKNOWLEDGMENTS

Sitting down to write this section of the book gives me a small sense of compassion for those folks who win the Oscar and want to ramble on and on about all the people in their life they want to recognize, knowing there simply isn't enough time or memory to be able to touch them all. As have they, I am sure I will miss a few along the way, and if I do, please forgive me. You are in my heart even if my head is too scattered to remember.

Thank you, thank you, thank you to those of you who have followed this journey for so long and who encouraged me and believed in me even when I struggled to see the wisdom you saw.

Thanks especially to Carrie Ure for all her editing and patience and sincere commitment to this project. No one would be holding this book in their hands were it not for Carrie's dedication.

Thanks to Julie Vaillancourt, Jeff VandenHoek, Cliff Hunter, Cheri Wasco, Jim Steele, Andreas Gast, and Craig Savage, the first eyes to see and review this work. Your honesty, your patience, your support and your time are much appreciated.

Thank you to my parents, Bob and Jackie Fulmer and my

in-laws, Wayne and Susan Nelson, for your encouragement and for not giving up on me. Mom, I guess you were right all along. You told me when I was young that one day I would write a book. Who'd a thunk it?

Lastly and most importantly I want to acknowledge my family. My wife Julia, whom I love with all my heart, without you I would not have had the courage and confidence to keep writing. You have been my soul mate since the moment I laid eyes on you. Each time you look at me with eyes that say "You are special," I am able to believe in myself a little more. Because of you, I get to be a better version of myself. Thank you for that.

As for my daughters – Sarah, who sees me the way I want to be seen, and Leah, whose smile and unyielding happiness daily remind me to live life with the wonder and joy of youthful exuberance – without them, what would be the point? The bumper sticker says, "I want to be the person my dog thinks I am!" I'm not sure what my dog thinks, but I want to be the person my daughters think I am. I want to be the dad they deserve. Because of them I find strength and courage. They are my inspiration.

Thank you, to everyone who believes in me.

Steven Fulmer
February 2012
Portland, Oregon

PART I

FREEING THE ANGEL

"I saw the angel in the marble and I carved until I set him free."

— Michelangelo

INTRODUCTION

This is a book about life, courage and possibility; a collection of vignettes, thoughts, stories and ponderings around the theme of personal and professional leadership. I have taken some liberties along the way, especially with regards to sailing references. I love sailing and believe it to be one of life's greatest metaphors. As the old adage says, "You can't change the wind, but you can adjust your sails." In other words, how we respond to life matters. The choices we make matter. What we allow to influence our thinking matters. Sailing teaches us that we can use a force doggedly determined to blow us away from our goal and transform it into the very power to propel us forward toward our destination.

I haven't written this book to give you permission to stop thinking, to simply follow what I say, should you decide that you agree with me. Nor am I suggesting that you find all the ways to pick it apart. Instead, use this book as inspiration to think, to challenge, to question and to choose. The question to ask yourself while reading is not, "Do I agree?" Instead, ask yourself what you will choose and then choose it!

This book is my attempt to change the world, to plant the seed of the novel idea that leadership and success don't need to catalyze greed in our world, but can engender solutions instead. I believe a significant measure of successful leadership is more a reflection of how we behave towards others, than it is the goals we have accomplished.

When we define leadership from a more global and humanitarian perspective; when we turn our vast intellect and creativity to what can be instead of what was; when we realize that the battle isn't with one another, but with the internal forces, voices and tendencies within us; we begin to understand that, in fact, we are all on the same human team, trying together for the larger trophy of success, happiness and well-being. We would do well to see more people as partners than adversaries. It's a realization that can change the game.

I recall an old Oprah episode celebrating the life of a garbage collector retiring after more than thirty years on the same route. He never wanted to be more or less than a garbage collector. He loved his job and it showed. On his last day, neighbors along his entire route came out to celebrate and honor him, telling stories of his interactions with their kids and recalling the kind things he had done on the job.

We don't all want the same thing. For those of us who want wealth, we should go for it, so long as we allow others to achieve *their* level of success, happiness and well being along the way. In the immortal words of Zig Ziglar, *"You will get all you want in life if you help enough other people get what they want."* To take it one step further; leadership also demands of us the courage and ability to recognize what success means to others in this world, and to help *them* be who they want to be.

Does that mean some will take advantage of the system? Probably. But instead of keeping score, we can embody a better way through our own intelligent leadership.

Too many leaders today think they need to scare the hell out of everyone to get the power to carry out their vision. In reality, we would all gain exponentially more power by helping people feel good and laugh more!

This book is about that kind of leadership.

FREEING THE ANGEL

When interviewed one day about his great gift of sculpting, Michelangelo was asked how he created such beautiful works of art. He replied, *"In every block of marble I see a statue as plain as though it stood before me, shaped and perfect in attitude and action. I have only to hew away the rough walls that imprison the lovely apparition to reveal it to the other eyes as mine have seen it."*

Once you get *your* clarity, are you willing to keep chiseling? Be prepared. The answer just might be no, and that's okay. The no is telling you that you have a great and detailed vision; you just haven't chiseled away enough to see the angel yet.

What you seek is already within you, in perfect form and attitude. The goal is therefore not *creation*, it's *revelation*, that is, information revealed. The goal is to uncover what is already there inside, to chip away at the rough walls – including self doubt, judgment, frustration, disappointment, guilt, shame or perhaps unworthiness – that have built up over time, imprisoning the lovely vision; to remove anything that isn't the angel, anything that isn't your vision. Only then can you and the rest of the world see what already exists.

To get there you must first see the vision of the angel within the rock. Then only *you* can chip away at the stones that imprison your vision. Only *you* can reveal the work of art that is waiting within you to come out and grace the rest of us. But I must warn you. To truly reveal this miracle will take an act of heresy. (I'll explain more later!)

Michelangelo also said, *"The greater danger for most of us lies not in setting our aim too high and falling short; but in setting our aim too low, and achieving our mark."*

Or to borrow a nautical metaphor, how high are you willing to raise your sails? You can be meek, humble, afraid others might see you, and raise them only halfway. Or are you willing to raise them all the way, high enough to give them shape, high enough to reach the top of the mast? Raising your sails only halfway up the forestay may be doable, but you cannot sail a ship that way.

The clearer your vision, the higher your sail. Are *you* willing to reach as high as it takes?

EVERYONE IS A LEADER

Everyone is a leader in the same way that everyone is an artist. We all have within us the capacity to be happy, successful and vibrant. In other words, each of has the in-born capacity to create art, just as each of us has the innate capacity to lead. The problem for most of us is that this potential is buried deep within, covered by mountains of fear, beliefs, judgments, doubt, past experiences and other people's fears, expectations and doubts. Revealing ourselves, *that* is our goal in leadership, just as in art. Uncovering the leader within is then partially about discovery and partially about creation and the secret lies in the balance.

You see, leadership isn't about the *right* way; it's about *your* way. And the best leadership books are less about the rules, guidelines and answers regarding leadership, and more about the questions they pose, the way they make you think and feel, how they tap into your inner core to help you determine the kind of leader you want to be, the kind of leader *you* choose to be.

Leadership isn't about following someone else's formula – that's following! The lessons you learn from others can serve only as peaks you climb to reach a higher vantage point for dreaming bigger, seeing further and achieving more than has ever been done before.

Leadership is about blazing your own trail, about how *you* want to be, as a unique individual among humanity.

THE WELL PLAN

I spend a lot of my time as a business and life coach dealing with people's obstacles, the things standing in their way preventing them from being, doing or having what they want. Some people call them excuses, but I find that to be such a negatively charged word. I prefer the word obstacles because they are things that literally stand in our way, things that we must get over, dive under, bust through or navigate around in order to get where we are going. A vast majority of the time when we encounter an obstacle, we look in the wrong direction for a solution. Mostly, we look *at* the obstacle and hope to see the solution there. Instead, when faced with a seemingly insurmountable problem, to find a solution I look at what happened right before the obstacle appeared.

Let me illustrate.

Let's say your goal is to clean your daughter's bedroom. You might think, "I just have to do it! It's not rocket science; it's just willpower."

And if I were to ask you the simple question, "What is preventing you from cleaning her room?" you might say, "Me. That's what. I just need to do it."

My natural reply, in the immortal words of Nike, would be,

"Then just do it."

And that's where it begins – The Well Plan.

"Well, I can't just jump in, I mean, it will take hours. I have to have the time."

"Oh, so doing it isn't actually the obstacle in the process, is it? Finding the anticipated number of available hours is the obstacle, which, you will notice, comes first, before the objective, not next to or after it."

"Well yes," you reply, "I just don't have the time. Where do I find the hours?"

"What do you have to do to schedule the time?"

"Well, obviously I need to look at my calendar."

"Where is your calendar?"

"Well, I don't have it with me."

"Oh, so the next step is actually finding your calendar. In other words, looking at your calendar isn't as obvious as you thought."

"Well (there's that word again!), yes, but I already know I don't have a block of time large enough."

So you can see it coming, can't you? The next question:

"What do you have to do to open up a large enough block of time?"

"Well, (and there it is again!) I will need to reschedule or cancel something."

"What are you willing to cancel or reschedule?"

"Well, I don't' know…"

And the conversation goes on until, well, until we get at the root of the issue and get crystal clear on what exactly is the true obstacle standing in your way today, right now. As we delve deeper and deeper we clear out the cobwebs and obstacles (i.e. excuses) that stand in your way. Ultimately we will get to the root of what you really want. We may find in the end that you don't *want* to clean your daughter's room. You want *her* to do it. However the obstacles in the way of getting her to do it are much bigger in your eyes than actually doing it yourself. But because you don't actually *want* to do it yourself, the obstacles standing in your way of doing anything at all loom large.

Well, what are you going to do about that?

What's *your* Well Plan? When you keep going deeper into the "well" you begin to see that neither the obstacles nor the objectives provides the answers. What comes before them often does. Many leaders fail to acknowledge the Well Plan, especially when they are leading themselves, their kids, or any group on anything *they don't really want to do*. To many this feels like psychobabble and a waste of time. "It's faster to just push through," I often hear it said. This would be true if you would actually push through and do it, but most don't, and obstacles stand strong while many a task, goal, responsibility or objective lies uncompleted on the to-do list from hell.

WHAT ARE YOU WILLING TO DO?

No one can tell you what to do. Just look at the obesity problem in our country. There are plenty of resources and voices out there telling us how to exercise and what to eat for better health, but do most of us do it? No. Why not? Because we don't want to! We may want some aspect of better health and fitness, but we don't want it all. At least, we aren't willing to work that hard or make that kind of sacrifice in order to have it. Which brings us back around to the questions at hand:

What do you want?

Describe with clarity your vision/goal/purpose/dream.

What do you mean when you say, "I want to be a better leader of self or others," "I want to be healthier," "I want to be a better Dad or Mom?"

It's the lack of clarity that holds people back more than any other single factor. And the reason for the lack of clarity is that once people start to get clear about what they want, they begin bumping up against that which they are unwilling to do.

Once you get really clear, the next question begins begging for an answer.

"What I am willing to do to get it?"

Many people who come to me for coaching know what they want. Some just aren't willing to do what they think it takes to get it.

LEADERSHIP IS HERESY

S omebody's got to say it, so it might as well be me.

Leadership is an act of heresy! Anything less is not leadership.

Now I know what you're probably thinking because when I say this in public I get all kinds of reactions. Some are quite offended, as if somehow this goes against their moral code. Often their jaws drop with that look of shock that says, "What? Heretics are those anarchist deviants who got burned at the stake in the Middle Ages. Heretics are the ones who break the rules, who go against the established norm, who act in defiance of the church or state. No way, no how, uh uh, that is *not* the kind of leader I want to be. This guy is a quack!"

Others give a slow cockeyed nod, a rebellious look in their eye that says, "Heretic! Yeah, cool! I like the sound of that!" When I open a speech by asking who is a heretic, these folks will raise their hands with enthusiasm. They also see a heretic as a bit of an anarchist, but to them that's a more positive thing than a negative one. When asked to define the term, however, they will say largely the same things as the first group.

"Aren't heretics the ones who break the rules, who go against the established norm, who act in defiance of the church or state?"

Then there are those in the audience who gaze back at me with the blank stare, a look of total confusion. They're wondering what in the heck I am talking about and whether this is some kind of trick.

The truth is that heresy *does* have a bad reputation, acquired back in the dark ages when the Church removed, imprisoned, or burned at the stake anyone who questioned or challenged its authority. Deeming those brave or foolhardy souls as heretics forever cemented in people's minds the idea that heresy is somehow bad.

Yet if you go back to its original intention and meaning, heresy is something quite different. The word comes from the ancient Greek and has a simple two-word definition: to choose. Heresy is the act of choosing! Therefore, a heretic is simply one who chooses instead of merely following. It doesn't take a rocket scientist to understand why the ancient powers-that-be "chose" to condemn those who would choose something different from the established way of thinking. But today, the mere act of disagreement, the presence of curiosity, the willingness to ask the bold questions about the status quo, while potentially threatening to those in power, is anything but bad.

Leadership is an act of heresy because it requires the courage to choose. I believe that most failed leaders fail to lead simply because they fail to choose. In doing so, they choose to follow.

Now before we get caught up in an argument of semantics, lets get clear. Is it possible to be a leader who chooses to follow a pre-existing doctrine?

Yes!

When running for public office, for example, a leader might choose to be a Republican or a Democrat. Or one could be the leader of a church and, with all her heart, buy into the doctrine of her faith. Just because one agrees with something that has come before and chooses the same, that does not somehow negate the possibility of being a heretical leader. Only if one fails to question the premises and controversies of his political party, faith-based religion, or scientific stance does he run the risk of squandering his leadership. Only if he fails to seek a deeper and clearer understanding of his group's doctrine or fails to challenge a doctrine that no longer serves, does he refuse the heretic's mantle.

One who simply carries out another's vision as his own, without question, clarification or challenge, is not a heretic and not a leader. He is a follower.

INSPIRED LEADERSHIP

Actions are born of your thoughts and visions. Is the clarity you are developing enough to inspire yourself and others? This is no trivial question.

The word inspire – meaning "to breathe in" – works well for leadership. Does the scope and clarity of your vision make others catch their breath? Does your leadership breathe life into what is possible for others as they rise up to a new level of themselves?

As both a coach and a man in love, I have struggled deeply with people who say that their partners "complete them," as if they were somehow half a person before. I secretly wonder which half they were, whether left, right, top, bottom, inside, outside, front, or back? They weren't walking around with only the left or right side of their body, when they suddenly met the other half walking around, fell in love, joined sides and lived happily ever after. Clearly we know this isn't true.

No. In fact, we're all whole and complete just they way we are. Yet sometimes when we meet someone special we are inspired to be an even better version of ourselves. We aren't completed so much as enhanced and perhaps, self-empowered, to be the best we can be.

After exploring this concept with many people, what has become clear to me is not that inspired individuals are suddenly made whole, but that through the eyes of the one they love or admire, they start to see themselves as others have seen them all along. They start to experience themselves as someone who is competent, talented, attractive, lovable.

The real gift we receive from those who love us is not their love, although that's a beautiful bonus. The real gift is the ability to experience ourselves as never before, to see in ourselves what we haven't seen. When I finally fell truly in love, I knew it was different because around my partner I was a better version of me than I had ever been before.

On the professional level, true leaders have the same power as our beloved. True leaders inspire. True leaders connect. True leaders open a space that allows us the freedom to step into our talents and gifts in a new and powerful way. In the presence of a genuine leader people *want* to step up. When we experience another who believes in us, who sees our angel within, we are free to be a better version of ourselves. Not completed, but enhanced!

On a personal level, those who choose to lead themselves have the courage to look in the mirror and risk seeing what they have never believed: that they are capable of so much more than they give themselves credit for. Once a true leader of self recognizes that she is capable, smart, talented and creative, she is then in a position to professionally inspire others.

PART II

THREE DIMENSIONS OF LEADERSHIP

"If you cannot find it in yourself, where will you go for it?"

— Confucius

I WISH IT WERE TRUE

I wish it were true, really I do. I wish the trickle down theory worked in business management. You know what I'm talking about, right? It's the economic principle that says, if you give tax breaks to corporations the savings will trickle down altruistically in the form of additional jobs, increased wages and better working conditions for those lower down on the socioeconomic ladder.

What if leadership worked the same way? What if we trained leaders at the top and their newfound skills trickled down throughout the entire organization, creating a better culture for all. If only that were true, as well! Unfortunately, too often organizations invest heavily in their C-suite and upper management, only to find that the results don't yield the benefits they seek. Why not?

I call it the telephone theory. Remember the game we played in a giant circle as kids? Someone whispered a secret to the person next to them and they in turn whispered it to the person next to them and so on. By the time the message got around to the person who originated it, things sounded dramatically different. It's like taking a copy of an image, then a copy of the copy, and then a copy of the copy's copy. With each iteration, the image degrades a little more. The same thing happens in business. Leadership gets degraded when we expect executives to learn and develop their skills and then go home and propagate their newfound knowledge. What they end up propagating is their vision and their own version of leadership.

Don't get me wrong; it is important and imperative for leaders to relay their visions. But once people learn how to lead, they generally step into the role, investing very little time or effort in teaching those underneath them how to engender leadership in themselves. Some think they need only *be* a great leader; others will simply learn from their behavior and duplicate the magic. For others, such mentoring might even be a threat. Still others never give a moment's thought to teaching others to lead.

Organizations that *do* cultivate leadership at every level of their operation – from their top-tier management teams all the way down to the workers on the assembly line – will not only survive, they will thrive. In the process they will transform whole companies, industries, and cultures. These forward-thinking organizations will discover that enhancing leadership at all levels takes more than a little trickle-down. It takes Three Dimensional Leadership.

LEADERSHIP IS THREE DIMENSIONAL

Traditionally the three dimensions of our universe are height, width and depth. Likewise, leadership is three-dimensional.

The First Dimension is the leadership of others through authority.

Great leaders are great for a number of reasons, but above all it is because they lift people up to a height unreachable on their own. Even though a leader can create a vision and paint the picture in such a way that others want to follow, one person's vision cannot be fulfilled without the buy-in, support and engagement of others. Even great leaders themselves cannot reach their highest heights completely on their own.

Steve Jobs is a pinnacle example of this dimension. With his gifts for seeing what others miss and creating needs where no one else even saw problems, he was the epitome of a visionary. Take the Apple product, the iPad, for example. The world wasn't clamoring for the iPad. In fact, mere mortals like me couldn't even have imagined such a thing. But Jobs did, and he created one of the great disruptive technologies of the decade.

According to his authorized biographer, Walter Isaacson,

Jobs painted the vision and then wielded his authority to will into being many of the innovative products that made Apple the world-wide phenomenon it is today. By all accounts, Jobs was a strong First Dimensional Leader,

In the First Dimension, people will tolerate a great deal from their leaders, provided they deliver the goods. Such was the case with Jobs. In its portrayal of Jobs following his death, Newsweek pointed out that he was a master of psychological manipulation, legendary for playing both good cop and bad cop. His colleagues put up with his temper and unpredictability, never sure if they were about to receive harsh criticisms or lavish praise. People followed Jobs because he was brilliant and because he had good ideas and he implemented them. They submitted to such unpredictability not only because he was a genius and they wanted to go where his vision was heading. He was also the boss!

Jobs' subordinates didn't question his authority to lead. As the appointed CEO of Apple, he was in the position to challenge people, and challenge them, he did. But he also had a gift for bringing out their best; for getting them to think in ways they never knew possible; for encouraging them to find unconventional solutions. Steve Jobs embodied the ability to take authority, to hold the position at the helm, and to lift oneself and others up to what is possible.

First Dimensional authority, the most common and most easily perceived of the three dimensions, is how most people see leadership. And yet far too many potentially great leaders fail because they stop there. They think that being the boss, having the authority, is all it takes to be the next Steve Jobs.

THE SECOND DIMENSION: LEADERSHIP OF SELF

In many keynote presentations and workshops, I ask audience members to raise a hand if they are currently a leader. Now let me make it clear, I am not asking if they hold a leadership title, have authority, or are in any way the official boss. I simply ask if they are a leader. With few exceptions, only those with a title or traditional position of leadership usually raise their hands.

When I follow up the question by asking what the others in the room are, if not leaders, it is surprising how few people have an answer. A few will say "follower." Others will venture forth a more positive label such as "team member" or "supporter." Many really don't know what they are, but they know what they aren't. They aren't leaders.

This couldn't be further from the truth.

A Sunday school lesson teaches that one cannot love another until he first learns to love himself. Well, the same is true for leadership.

One cannot lead others if one cannot first lead oneself.

For those in leadership roles, especially those who are successful and effective, this will sound a bit obvious. For those aspiring to leadership and wondering why they haven't achieved it themselves, this will likely be met with a "humph!" Many will push against the aphorism as lame or "duh" but won't really grasp it. The truth eludes many people because it's a version of leadership that eliminates external blame. Yet neither does it turn the blame inward. It simply shifts responsibility.

After all, it's easy to ascribe responsibility to those who make the big bucks. They have the authority and the reward, and as the old saying goes, *"With the gravy goes the grief."* Assigning responsibility to them is easy.

Turning it inward, however, is a different story altogether.

"When I'm not the one in control of my life," you might say, "how can I assume full responsibility? I don't set the hours I need to be at work. I don't determine the abundant workload. I can't choose what to do and when to do it. For the aspects of my life in which I am in control, I will gladly take full responsibility. But I cannot take full responsibility for the idiocy of my boss."

Okay, I'll buy that you can't take responsibility for your boss. But you *can* take full responsibility for yourself.

The question isn't, "How can I change *them*?" The question is, "How can I control how *I* choose to respond?"

Just because you think your boss is a jerk doesn't mean you have to be upset by him. You could let it slide. You could quit. You could change the environment. You could even invoke the Third Dimension of Leadership – influence. But before we go there, let's wrap up the Second Dimension with a twist.

People often interpret the Second Dimension in one of two ways. Some assume that the Second Dimensional Leader has nothing to do with the First Dimensional Leader, i.e. the one with the title and authority. Others, often the ones *with* the title and authority, look at the Second Dimension and say, "See! It doesn't matter *what* I do. You are responsible for yourself! Get over it and get to work!"

In the former interpretation, people can feel isolated, alone and having nowhere to turn. Either I lead with authority or I lead only myself, they opine.

In the latter interpretation, First Dimensional Leaders can end up using the Second Dimension as a club to beat, threaten or emotionally abuse others. Clearly neither of these interpretations is healthy.

In reality, these Three Dimensions aren't separate leaders. They are all one. Just as every three-dimensional building has height, width *and* depth, every leader has all three. When leaders realize that the height of their leadership is their vision, but the width of their leadership is their people, they begin to look at the Second Dimension as the realm of empathy and connection.

As a leader, once you recognize that others have trouble stepping into their own level of leadership, you realize that there is a role you can play in assisting them. The more you observe others, the more you understand that most people in this world don't need to be right. Most people just want to be heard. They want to be seen, validated, and recognized. They want anything but to be invisible.

The more people feel validated, the more they can step into their own leadership, and the more they can take responsibility for their own decisions, choices and responses. Many people can't do this on their own. So when a leader of others begins to recognize *within herself,* how she was able to do this for herself, she is more likely to get in touch with the emotional impact of the journey. She will naturally begin to help others along the process, or at the very least, create an environment in which her people can thrive and discover their own leadership within. And the more she creates such an environment, the more people she will attract to her team who are self-leaders – validated, recognized, and courageous enough to step up and risk having their own vision. These Second Dimensional team members will also be more likely to find ways to connect their personal vision with that of the team. Once *that* happens, anything is possible.

Every person on the team has the potential to step into this Second Dimension. Once they do, they are a stronger, more committed and viable member of the organization. We all know that a wider base is more stable than a narrow one. Build a wide base of Second Dimension Leaders and there is no telling what heights your vision will reach.

What is standing in the way of *your* personal leadership? Where are you giving away your authority and responsibility?

What is the one thing that, if you were to change it, would have the greatest impact on your ability to lead yourself?

THE THIRD DIMENSION:
LEADERSHIP THROUGH INFLUENCE

The Third Dimension is leadership *without* authority.

Now, if you take a board and cut it wide enough to hold the number of team members stepping into their own leadership and connecting their vision to the vision of the team; then you cut it high enough to reach up to the heights of your vision, way up there among the stars of possibility, it still won't stand up on its own. That's because for anything to stand on its own requires the third dimension – depth. The deeper the leadership, the more stable the leadership. It's that simple.

Business guru Jim Collins simply asks, *"Will they follow you even when they don't have to?"* As any volunteer organization will likely confirm, the most difficult – and powerful – form of leadership is where you have all of the responsibility to carry out a vision, with none of the authority to make it so. You can't use the excuse, "Because I said so, and I'm the boss, that's why!" when your team is all volunteers. The Third Dimension of Leadership is leadership through influence.

Many career counselors and coaches will ask, "What would you do, if you could do anything? What is the one thing that you love to do so much that you would do it for free?"

This is what the Third Dimension is like. If you take the tool (or crutch) of authority out of the equation, what's left? What do you use to motivate, educate, empower, connect and drive your team?

In employment studies, it will likely not surprise you that money and compensation packages are not the leading determinants of a person's engagement in their job. In fact, of the top four determinants, salary comes in fourth, and a distant forth at that. Before money comes number three, doing meaningful work that aligns with ones talents and skills. Number two is relationships with one's peers. The number one element contributing to high levels of employee engagement is the relationship with one's boss!

So I ask the question again, how will you motivate, educate, empower, connect and drive your team?

You will build relationships.

It turns out that how you manage your relationships is not just a question for your personal life; it's a question for your professional life as well.

Patrick Lencioni, in *The Five Dysfunctions of a Team*, writes that the job of a sports coach is to create the best team possible, not to foster the careers of the individual athletes. I only partially agree with that. In calling out the team, too many leaders and coaches forget that the team is only an abstract entity. Take away the people and there is no such thing as a team. It's just an empty vessel.

Moreover, if you change any of the members, you change the dynamics of the team. Just as one arrogant, selfish renegade can bring down the morale and spirit of the rest of the participants, a powerful leader, even just one of the players who has a phenomenal attitude, can light up the team.

The individual matters, and the cultivation of that individual matters as well.

Jack Welch once said, *"The teams with the best players win!"* But that's not always true. The teams with the individuals who play best *together*, who are out to succeed, regardless of who gets the credit, and who are willing to let their teammate take the winning shot – they win most!

In fact, as recounted in Michael Lewis' book, *Moneyball,* the Oakland Athletics baseball team is a case in point. In 2002, rather than paying big money for individual talents, the A's general manager Billy Beane began to evaluate and draft players based on their ability to contribute to the team's wins. His unorthodox strategy enabled the A's to win more games than teams buying the best players and out-spending their payroll three-to-one. Not only did the A's finish in the play-offs, they eventually pulled-off the longest winning streak in baseball history. Why? Because Beane recognized that the secret to success lies in capitalizing on *every* individual's strength; not just being your personal best, but being willing to fit your best into the larger entity.

As a leader, you have the dual responsibility to cultivate

the individual and her dreams, goals and objectives, as well as a team culture that allows the particular collection of individuals to come together to play for something bigger than themselves. Individuals have strengths and weaknesses. The goal isn't to deny the weaknesses, but to bolster the strengths that contribute to the team's overall goals. You can think about it this way: it is the team, not its individuals, that is well rounded.

As a general rule, we are selfish creatures with an innate sense of self-preservation imperative to our existence. The key to building great teams is to use the Second and Third Dimensions of Leadership to build great individuals, individuals who can clearly and powerfully align their own vision, with the larger mission of your leadership. So long as your players are participating just for a paycheck, they will never be loyal and committed team members. However, once they connect with you on a personal level, then leadership transcends obligation and moves into commitment. Build personal relationships with your team members and they will either align with your vision or make room for someone who will.

When you start to look at the Three Dimensions of Leadership, you begin to realize they are all interconnected. You can't lead yourself or others without a compelling vision that lifts people up to a world of what is possible. And you can't effectively lead a group of people who cannot effectively lead themselves.

People need to be anchored to their own dreams and definitions of success in order to give their all to something bigger than themselves. When *you* have a clue of what that is for others and can influence them to connect to the larger world around them, that's the Third Dimension, the realm where everyone raises their visions of themselves, where everyone is more than they can be on their own.

THE IMPORTANCE OF VISION

I don't get much argument on this one. Every leader I have ever addressed has agreed with the importance of their vision. They are fond of saying, "If you don't know where you are going, how are you going to get there?"

Fair enough. But I'd like to phrase it a bit differently: "If you don't know where you are going, how will you know when you have arrived?"

There is an important, if subtle difference in these questions that relates more to what your team hears. The first statement focuses primarily on the "how," that is, the doing, while the second focuses on the "what" you've set out to achieve. The big difference is that the one sees people as tools while the other invites them in as partners to a solution.

Remember that your vision is what empowers your people. If you only dole out information about how to get there, they feel more like they are being told rather than invited. More importantly, without a clear picture of the end game, people don't see the whole picture and they don't know how to contribute. If they can't envision what it will look like when they arrive, they can't prepare and they can't pace themselves. Wouldn't you rather know whether you are running a half marathon, a full marathon or a triathlon?

We live in a Nike frame of mind. The eloquent motto "Just Do It!" has brainwashed us into believing that "doing" is the key. It doesn't matter *what* we do, I have had people tell me. Just doing something is better than nothing. Action is always better than inaction. In this context the rhetorical question many leaders pose about *how* to get there makes perfect sense.

But what you really want, I would argue, is to paint such a detailed picture about what it looks like *once you arrive* that people can't wait to get there. In fact when they know the target destination, when they can imagine feeling the sun on their face, and fantasize tasting the sweetness of victory, your team may well find creative new "how's" to achieve the goal more efficiently than you could ever imagine as their leader.

THE THIRTY-INCH VIEW

As a leader – whether we're talking about taking control over your own life, or leading a corporate or non-profit team of superstars – you want it all: a vision as lovely and inspiring as a Rembrandt with all the detail of an architectural blueprint. The more your followers understand what the Promised Land looks and feels like, the better. Leadership isn't the time for abstraction; it's the time for clarity.

To use a sailing analogy, we can't travel with the sail at half-mast; it doesn't function that way. Even during a gale when we choose to put up a much smaller storm jib, we must still raise-up the sail completely and allow it to stretch to its full capacity. Raising the sail isn't just a romantic ideal; it's a deliberate choice, an act of power, a statement of intent. And just as one can't be half pregnant, out on the voyage of human relations, we can't just-sort-of raise our leadership sail; we are either heading toward our destination or we are lost at sea.

Raising your sail of leadership is not only about magic and wonder and dreams. It's also about the detail. Not a 30,000-foot level of detail, but a thirty-inch level of detail. At 30,000 feet the world looks at peace and the land looks whole. But when you get down to ground level, reality tells a different story altogether. At thirty inches we see the scratches, the cracks, the nuances and the variances. As followers, this is the level of detail we seek.

Yes, we need pie-in-the-sky idealism, the-world-is-our-oyster speeches as well. Even before we set sail, we can feel the forces of the wind creating power, wanting to create the lift necessary for propelling us into the world of possibilities. We need the exhilaration we feel as the sails begin to rise and the wind begins to snap and whip the giant cloth.

Yet as wonderful and exciting as that emotion is, if we were to lift the sail only halfway and just luxuriate in the initial feeling of exhilaration, we would find that it's simply lots of noise without any real control. At some point we have to continue, beyond the place of transition and momentum, to raise the sails of our dreams and visions, and inflate them with more details and practical specifics. This is precisely where some leaders fall short.

I am a huge Barack Obama admirer. During the 2008 presidential campaign, I loved his speeches about hope and possibility and reaching across the aisle. He filled his listeners with all the excitement of that hope as he spoke. It was loud and exhilarating and we could feel it deep down inside; we could feel the wind starting to fill the sail that would propel the boat forward. We knew that once we set sail, great things would happen.

As of this writing, Obama is in the midst of his second

presidential campaign, and we are faced with the knowledge that to fully inflate his sail of leadership in a second term will require dealing with all kinds of forces, including the economy, partisan politics, the other campaigns, and his approval rating among the voters. To raise presidential leadership full-mast, Obama will need to convince the American public with the working details of his vision.

Mind you, the goal in leadership isn't to remove your opposition; no matter what you do, some forces will always blow against you. You don't change them. Rather, the goal is to convert the raw energy into power and solution. Obama will never convince the Republican Party to sanction increased government spending any more than conservatives will ever convince staunch liberals to adopt their social agendas. Yet the energy of the dialogue has the power to inspire millions to get off the couch on Election Day.

Those who are your followers, your crew, your team, they must believe in the possibility of your vision *after* the excitement of the 30,000-foot level speech has faded. Remember, knowledge and excitement have a half-life. By the time people leave the room where they've heard your speech they have forgotten most of it. By the time they get to their car, even more has dripped out of their ears. In the real world, after we feel the excitement of raising the sail, leadership lives and dies by the details. "Alright," you may say. "I've just given my 30,000-foot sail-raising speech and people are excited. Now what?"

That's when many leaders drop into judgment. They face the obstacles in their way and they ask the question, "How am I going to obliterate those obstacles and achieve my goal? What am I going to *do*?"

When starting with a high-level vision leaders can fool themselves into believing that is *all* they need to do. It sounds like this: "Here's my vision. Keep it short, keep it sweet, keep it simple and everyone will be on board. If they're not, they will be made available to industry and I will bring in people who *do* believe."

The problem with this reasoning is that many of their people already *do* believe. Such leaders just don't know it yet. They see questions, doubts, and objections as mutiny rather than insight. Instead of using their people's opposition as power, leaders simply try to eliminate it. As a result, they lose the real energy available to them.

Opposition is a lot like the principle Thomas Edison spoke of when he said, *"Opportunity does not knock but once upon your door; it pounds constantly, but it's dressed in overalls and looks like work!"*

True leadership and the courage to face opposition *can* be a lot of work. I have had many a client come to me to become a leader, only to go down a different path because they weren't interested in the amount of work necessary to achieve the goal. What we soon find out, however, is that no matter whether we choose to be a leader of others, we are always a leader of ourselves and the same rules apply. And even in leading our own lives we face opposition. Attempting to bend everyone we meet to our own way of thinking, we soon tire of the task. Eventually we find that peace, joy, happiness and success more rapidly come our way when, like Thomas Edison, we recognize opportunity in the tools, gifts and insights others bring to the party, even when it feels like a contradiction. If we remember that the wind must blow across – not with – the sail to create lift, we will not just tolerate, but desire, invite, and seek opposition.

CLARITY, COURAGE AND CHANGE

How will you know when you've arrived? Let's illustrate with a personal example.

Introduced to me through a mutual friend, a client comes to me with a vision of starting a whitewater rafting company. It's a dream Chuck has had since he was sixteen years old. Everyone around him is opposed to the idea and no one is afraid to tell him so. After all, he has a fantastic job, making great money. He has outstanding flexibility to come and go as he pleases. The problem is that no one else seems to understand the importance and value of his dream. So try as he may, Chuck is unable to garner the necessary support to embark on his project and he feels discouraged. He asks quite simply, "Can you help me fulfill my dream?" and he pours his heart out to me.

His story takes about fifteen or twenty minutes and it sounds exciting. When I then ask what the problem is, he says that he just doesn't know how to get there.

"I've got too many forces against me and I can't seem to find the strength and courage to make this happen. How do I make this happen?"

Ah, the dreaded How.

So we spent some time delving into the vision, exploring the obstacles and getting a clear image of what he was really battling. Over the weeks we kept coming back to his vision because, as I posed in the next set of questions, I perceived that he lacked only the clarity of detail. The 30,000-foot romantic version was solid: self-employment, the great outdoors, doing what he loves, teaching people to overcome fear, living on the river…the list was long and it sounded great. We needed only to bring it out of the clouds and work on the practicalities.

"How many hours a day are you working? How many employees do you have? What is your wife's role? What about your kids? (Keep in mind; he formed this dream in his teens, long before being married with children.) What will you do in the winter? Tell me about cash flow and retirement and growth in the business. How does your role grow and change?"

I asked these questions because the scope of his vision was limited, much of it based on an experience with the rafting company he worked for as a teen.

"Tell me about your dreams," I then said one day.

"What do you mean," he replied. "This *is* my dream."

"No," I said, "What about the other dreams? Surely your life isn't one hundred per cent about a rafting company. Tell me about your kids and fatherhood, your relationship with you wife and how that relationship grows over the years. What other dreams do you have? In other words, take me deeper into the whole picture of your life and what you value and what's important to you."

And over the weeks he did. Chuck was thirty-two years old when he came to me. He had held his dream for literally half his life. He knew what he wanted; he'd just never had enough specific details to move forward. However, together, we got there. And a whole vision showed up. The more specific he got, the more clearly focused his vision became. The more detailed his clarity, the more answers showed up. There was less and less wondering about how and where the courage would be coming from, because he now knew. And every time the vision led him down the slippery slope of judgment, we came back up for a deeper level of clarity. Decisions were getting easier, all the way to the moment when a major epiphany occurred and it came time for him to move into action.

The clearer Chuck got, the more he could see what it would look like when he arrived. As his longstanding vision merged with the other dreams in his life, Chuck no longer wanted to run a whitewater rafting company. When he really looked at the details, the impact on his life and life-style, his relationships with his children and his wife, the danger factor of whitewater rafting every day, and so much more, he began to realize that the vision he had wasn't the vision he wanted. A shift needed to occur.

What happens to so many leaders is that they make a statement about what they want or plan to achieve – on either the personal or professional level –and as the details pan out, they realize it isn't *exactly* what they want. But they continue to force it anyway. I suspect that has a lot to do with our society. (God forbid I ever get nominated to the Supreme Court because, horror of horrors, I have actually changed my mind about many things over the course of my lifetime. If you took a good look at my past you might find a contradiction or two.) Unfortunately, our society doesn't afford its leaders the luxury of growth and evolution, so it becomes incumbent upon leaders to grow and evolve on their own.

And that's exactly what happened with Chuck. After years of claiming that one day he would start a whitewater rafting business, he began to evolve. It turns out that everyone else had been right, if not for exactly the right reasons, and you can imagine how difficult that was for him to realize. He instantly became worried about the "I told you so's," and now he needed the courage to change his mind in the face of all the perceived judgments.

In short order Chuck found that courage and he made some big and bold decisions about his dreams. In the end he gave up none of them, he simply got more clarity about what it would be like when he arrived. As long as he was concerned how he was going to reach his vision, there was little room left for its evolution. It wasn't until we asked the question, "How will you recognize your arrival?" that he was able to really see it from a new perspective and gain the clarity he needed to step into his perfect life.

The irony is that outwardly Chuck changed very little about his work. He simply found a new way to bring in what he wanted from rafting: extended time outdoors with his family, exhilaration, and freedom. Instead of walking away from a thriving three-generation family business, he started catering to a new clientele, organizing outdoor trips, and inviting those around him to participate in his new vision in exciting ways. People rallied around him with support and engagement instead of criticizing the change to the vision.

That's the power of vision. That's the power of leadership through clarity. That's the power of asking how you will know when you have arrived. When you are crystal clear, and you can articulate your thirty-inch level of detail to your team and your community, not only will you more swiftly attain your goal, you will also inspire others to go after their own dreams. You will be amazed to see how often their goals align with your own.

PART III

GETTING PERSONAL

"You are the leader you've been waiting for."

— Maria Shriver

WHAT MAKES LEADERSHIP DIFFICULT

Leadership is difficult because it's hard work. Leadership is not for the weak of will or the inherently lazy. Leadership is for those who truly seek to make real and meaningful connections. Most people who want to call themselves leaders fail to lead. Instead it is easy to bark orders, bellow commands, and make edicts that are followed unquestioning. That's not leadership.

Real leadership, whether of self or of others, takes a concerted effort because real leaders meet people where they are, rather than where they wish them to be. You can wish all you want that your employees were more engaged, smarter, better problem solvers, better sales people, more of a team, willing to work longer hours. And yet, for all your wishing, the facts remain the same. They *are* where they are, with the skills, personalities, talents and abilities that they have. The good news is that it is not where they are going to stay.

Consider weight as an analogy. I am sure you will find it hard to believe that there was a time in my life when I tipped the scales at a whopping eight pounds. Yep, it's true, eight pounds! Can you believe it? When I think of how far I have come since those days it all feels like a distant memory, but it's true. Today I am more than seventeen times that weight! I'm an absolute giant in comparison to that time and yet, I am still considered quite small. How can that be? It's because everything is relative. And yet one changes.

As a leader, one of the most important lessons you can learn is that leadership is multi-leveled. At the macro level, it's like the team sport of competitive sailing in which the imperative is to pull together cohesively as a unit. As captain you realize that you can't have the starboard side of the boat moving in one direction and the port side doing something else. The keel and the rudder simply must work in unison or, well, you won't stay in the race. And yet, within that single hull sailboat are many parts working together, just as in business and in life there are many individuals making individual contributions and aligning with individual visions, dreams, and rules of fulfillment.

One size does not fit all, and the work of leadership is to meet each one of those individual entities one-on-one, connecting their reason for being on board with the bigger picture of the wind, the water and the race. Do that and you build loyalty, empower greatness and form a bond that goes beyond winning, money or even security.

How do you make those connections? By understanding values – yours *and* theirs. And by values, we aren't talking about those things we learned in Sunday school. You know, integrity, honesty and respecting your neighbor, all of which are beautiful, valid and necessary. We are instead talking about the daily benchmarks used to guide and govern our lives. We're talking about much deeper, more individualistic and esoteric values such as Sand Between My Toes.

SAND BETWEEN MY TOES

Years ago an unhappy young woman from the east coast I'll call Mary, came to me for personal and professional coaching. She had tried other routes to well being, including counseling, therapy, and guidance from her priest and close friends, all to no avail. By the time she finally called me, frustration and confusion filled her voice.

"I don't know what's wrong," Mary said. "For the last three years, life has been a downward spiral and I can't seem to stop it. I am less happy and seem more frustrated by the day and I can't seem to work my way out of this funk!"

After listening attentively I asked the obvious question, "What happened three years ago?"

"I've thought about that over and over," she said, "and the answer is nothing! I have the same job, the same husband, the same kids, the same car, the same route to work…"

With a soft chuckle I asked, "Is *that* the problem? *Nothing* has changed in the last three years?"

Smiling now, she thought for a moment and said, "No, I don't think so. I love those parts of my life. I wouldn't trade them for anything. It's not the big things, it's the little daily things that are always present, the stresses, the worries, the frustrations, the fears…nothing particularly horrible, just ordinary life stuff. It just seems to be affecting me more."

So we went to work. Over the next couple of weeks we explored many areas of her life, with little success. While we were able to touch on various individual events and see how each could improve, the collective whole of her happiness wasn't really changing. Mary still reported having last felt happy three years before.

It was time to take a different tack. I next helped Mary to explore her values with a simple and powerful tool I call The Values Timeline. (See Appendix II) After I explained the exercise, she dutifully accepted the task, allowing herself plenty of time to deeply explore the process. To my surprise, when she returned, it appeared that aliens had abducted her and left in her place an entirely different woman, one who was happy, cheerful, excited and full of energy.

"Holy cow! Mary, what happened?" I asked.

"You will never believe it," she said. "I did your exercise and I have to admit, for the first week and a half I thought it was pretty silly. I was doing it, but I wasn't getting anything from it. I stuck with it only because that was the commitment I made. As I started going back over it again and again, what I found was that I exhausted the list of events in my life pretty quickly. It's not like I was constantly remembering new things. Instead, every time I went back to the timeline, and asked what it was about each event that I valued, or what value was dishonored in a negative event, I managed to go a little deeper.

"Then suddenly a few evenings ago, I was looking at the timeline. Just looking, when I noticed something interesting. I saw a pattern as clear as day: roughly every six months I would go to the beach.

"As I thought back on the trips, which were seldom long, most down and back in the same day, it was the pattern that stood out. Trips to the beach almost always followed difficult events; if not tragedies, then at least stressful times. So I began to ask myself what I valued about these trips and it instantly became clear that my core value, something I value more than anything else, besides, perhaps, my kids, is the feeling of sand between my toes!

"There is something about walking barefoot in the sand. It doesn't matter what time of the year, whether summer, winter, hot, cold, as long as I can feel the sand between my toes it works. I can walk that way for hours, mindless of the time, just breathing the salty air as I feel the sand, smell the sea and connect with God. It has been these trips to the beach where I always find myself. It has been these trips to the beach that have connected me to my source. It has been during these trips to the beach that I have been able to release my stress, find my head and create clarity out of chaos. And guess when it was that I last went to the beach?"

"Hmm," I thought. "If I were to hazard a guess, I would

say, what, three years ago?"

"Yes! Exactly!"SO GUESS WHAT I DID THIS WEEK-END? GUESS!"

"Umm, you went to the beach?"

"Yes! It was fantastic! I walked for over six hours. Sometimes I would just walk and sometimes I would stop and just twist my feet into the sand to remember how it felt. Sometimes I would walk and meditate with an open, clear mind and sometimes I had long arguments with God.

"I value a lot of things in my life, Steven, but I've got to say, I value sand between my toes pretty much more than anything else, because as long as I have that, I can withstand anything. And believe it or not, I always knew that I loved it, but I never realized how I *valued* it and the significant role it plays in my life and well being."

MOVING BOULDERS

There's a story I once heard about a young boy and his father walking down a country lane. The boy, all of eleven or twelve years old, concentrated on the conversation, which was one of considerable depth and he was truly captivated by its possibilities. You see, the father was talking about what is possible when one has the courage to believe in and use all of one's power.

"Anything is possible, but you have to completely believe in and engage your power," his father repeated, driving home the point. The conversation wound around as conversations do with young boys who are alive and alert and easily distracted. As they walked along throughout the journey, the boy would round back again to the topic, challenging it from different perspectives.

"You mean, I could be president? An NBA star, even if I'm the shortest kid in my class? You mean, if I really believed in all my power, I could even have a baby?" he asked, giggling, as he already understood the birds and bees. His dad laughed along with him, but never said no.

Moments later they rounded a bend in the road and came upon a good-sized boulder in the middle of the path. Excited by its size the boy ran ahead to take a closer look. It was nearly as tall as he was. At first he was all boy, climbing on, over and around the boulder, when it eventually dawned on him.

"Dad," he asked, "are you saying that if I believe in and use all my power I could move this boulder?"

"Absolutely, son."

"Really?"

"Why not?" asked the dad. "If you truly believed in and used all your power, I know you could move that boulder."

So with a herculean grin the boy climbed down, got his shoulder up under it, dug in his heels and with all the power and faith he could muster, he attempted to move the boulder. It scarcely knew he was there. Straining with all his might, the boy gave it every ounce of strength he had to give, but the rock failed to move. The dad could see the sweat forming on the boy's brow as the smile began to fade and the effort slowed to a standstill.

"It's not true," the boy finally said, sadly. "I can't just believe my way into miracles."

"Hmm. Are you sure you used all your power, son?"

"Are you kidding me? I practically pulled my arms off!"

"True, you did give it everything you had to give, but did you use all your power?"

Confused, his son looked up, trying with as much effort to understand the question as he had used to move the rock.

"I don't understand."

"Son," said the dad, "I am part of your power and you didn't use me at all. What if you asked me for help?"

With a tinge of confusion as the significance of his father's words settled in, the boy asked, "Would you help me?"

"Absolutely!" And together they addressed the boulder and together they dug in their heels and together, with great effort, they rolled the rock away, off to the side of the road. The boy smiled, and you could see, just as the father did, that in the end he got it, clear and simple.

We only need to believe in and use all of our power, and just because *I* can't, doesn't mean *we* can't.

HOW MANY TIMES
DO I HAVE TO ASK YOU?

"How many times do I have to ask you to be quiet before you will actually BE quiet?"

There is absolutely no way any of us could have anticipated the supreme value of that question in the moment that it was asked.

It was, after all, one of the worst arrangements you could imagine for the circumstances. We were a group of two-dozen teens and a few chaperones invited to spend a couple of nights at a ski retreat at the Mt. Hood Mazama Lodge. Now the Mazamas are mountain climbers. Serious Mountain Climbers. Not gondola riders, not chair lift jockeys, not snow machine captains. They are real mountain climbers, which means they actually WALK up the face of mountains for fun!

Among the myriad things that make the Mazamas interesting is the fact that they built beautiful rustic lodges on mountains to give themselves a place to rest up before making their strenuous treks. They aren't hotels, these lodges. There aren't individual rooms with private showers and maids pulling back your blankets at night before placing exotic chocolates on your pillow. No, they are dorms with bunks, similar to what you might see in a work camp. Some are male. Some are female. Some rooms hold ten or twelve folks. Others hold twenty-five to thirty.

We were granted the privilege of inhabiting their lodge because we had a good friend, a card-carrying member of the Mazamas, who had vouched for us. For our part, we agreed to abide by the rules and respect the other guests. And one of the most important, most respected rules of the Mazama Lodge is the rule of silence. You see, Mazamas go to bed early – 8 or 9 p.m. – because they get up in the middle of the night to begin their ascent on Mt. Hood in order to reach certain elevations before the sun rises and makes the snow unstable. So, upstairs in the dorms, there is a silence rule that starts when the first person goes up to bed.

Did I mention I was with a group of teens?

When it finally came time to turn in, we were presented with the first real challenge. The two dorms that had been reserved for us – one male and one female – became occupied by some climbers who didn't get the message. That left only the one large dorm for our gang of boys and girls, adults and teens, all in the same room, with no way to adjust the bolted-in bunks to easily and comfortably accommodate the gender split. So we adults did our level best to whisper instructions to one another as we tried to corral the teens into an acceptable arrangement. We managed to do a pretty good job. At least no boys were in touching distance of any of the girls. And we considered that a success. Even better, we made all these arrangements with relatively little noise.

Then the lights went out.

Like popcorn, slowly at first and then more frequently as the situation heated up, the comments started popping. Each subsequent comment got a little louder, and soon the laughter began. That was okay at first because it was only a few comments over a few minutes. We adults felt good just shushing the teens as one would soothe an infant back to sleep. But as more time passed, instead of the comments dying down, they picked up, getting louder with each remark. One by one, the adults took their turns asking the teens to be quiet, reminding them to be respectful, imploring them to take it down a notch. You name it, we tried it. After each adult had taken a turn, some more than once, it became clear that *I* was expected to contribute to the effort.

I didn't know what to do. How does one change a crowd that is intent on moving in a particular direction? I certainly had no profound words of wisdom. So I just asked the question, "How many times do we have to ask you to be quiet before you will actually BE quiet?"

And the room went dead silent – for about four full seconds. Then some smart aleck spoke out the answer:

"SEVEN!"

The room erupted in tension-releasing laughter, over which I said, "Please be quiet," to no impact whatsoever.

"Please be quiet."

"Please be quiet."

"Please be quiet," and the laughter started dying down.

"Please be quiet," and it got a little quieter.

"Please be quiet," and all you could hear were a few murmurs.

And with a pregnant pause in my rhythm I said for the seventh time, "Please... be... quiet."

And they were, for the rest of the night. Not a peep.

All of us adults held our breath, waiting for the delayed uproar we were certain was about to follow, but it never came. None of us anticipated it would work, but it did, and I have used it countless times since, with kids, with adults, in business and with volunteer groups. The question is always a bit different. Sometimes it's "What will it take for you to do_____?" or "How many times are we going to do the same thing expecting a different result?" or "What is it, exactly, that is standing in your way?" And the list goes on.

The point is that the vast majority of the time, people know exactly what they need. The problem is that we leaders are often unwilling to ask the question, perhaps for fear of the answer. After all, what would I have done if the smart aleck in the Mazama Lodge had said 100, or 1,000 or a 1,000,000? I would have said, "That's unrealistic. Give me a more legitimate answer."

People want to engage and they want to be responsible, but like teens, we are so used to *not* being asked, not having a say in our lives, not being fully respected by the answer, that we don't often know how to behave.

I sincerely believe that it was because I gave those teenagers the choice and I simply delivered what they asked for, that we got what we wanted. I wasn't forcing, I was responding. More importantly, I invited them into the problem and the solution, instead of simply handing down an edict. I believe my question to the teens, simple and naïve, allowed the problem to take shape: a seven is more than a zero, but not as big as a seventy. It gave them power and it gave them the responsibility to both participate in the rule making and to follow the rule.

Are you inviting your team into the solution with questions that open up possibility, and participation? Or are you shutting them down and putting them on the defensive from the start? The types of questions you ask will make the difference, and "why questions" can be among the worst. For instance, the question "Why did you break the lamp?" presumes that the other person actually broke the lamp. She's guilty without a trial and all that remains unanswered is why she did it. As the recipient of such a question, your only recourse is to jump into defense mode and begin making your case. Instantly your reputation and privileges are on the line, you heart rate goes up, and your brain starts searching for strong, logical sentences that will support your case.

But if I ask the question differently, if I say, "How did the lamp get broken?" no assumptions are being made. Clearly the lamp is broken, as it is lying in pieces on the floor. Yet with a "how question," there is no need for defensiveness and a real dialogue can follow. By backing-off just a little, by not being so "in your face" I can open up possibilities for understanding.

In sailing, pulling the sails too tight is called over-sheeting and it can actually capsize a boat. By loosening the sails you can "dump air" and give the boat more flexibility. Similarly, by loosening the sail of understanding, leadership has the opportunity to lift others to a higher level of communication, clarity and participation. That will harnesses the energy of opposition and put it to good use drivine your boat forward.

PUSH VS. LIFT

Things are not always what they seem. If only I had a buck for every time *that* rang true in my life!

I grew up in Baltimore, Maryland on the majestic Chesapeake Bay and from the moment I could move all I wanted to do was go fast. So when my dad bought his first boat, I was thrilled. It was a cool blue open-bow tri-hull runabout that went so fast I thought my hair was going to blow off my head. As a six-year old speed-demon I loved the way that boat would lean into turns, the bow popping into the air when my dad thrust the throttle to full speed just before he trimmed the motor. Bam! The boat jumped over wakes and waves and, if there were none to be found, Dad would make a sharp banking turn so he could cross our own wake. My brothers and I thought that was just too cool for words.

Have I said that I loved speed? Faster boats would come screaming by our little runabout or small cabin cruiser, a boat we graduated to in later years. Those long sleek pointy-nosed cigarette boats grabbed my attention and started my little heart pumping. They were just too cool and everything I wanted. Yet every weekend I spent on the bay confused me just a little bit more.

Right in the middle of my drooling over something going faster than us, a pristine white sail would float mysteriously past us with a quiet confidence, pointing purposefully into the rich blue skies of a Maryland summer. I'd swear those sailboats winked as they glided by, taunting me. When the speedboats were long gone, it was the sailboats that left me mesmerized. It was their majesty and mystery, not their speed that enthralled me.

"How do they do that?" I asked. "I mean, I get it that the wind can blow them away, but how do sailboats get home again?"

It just didn't make sense to me, and it was probably the only question I ever asked during my youth that Dad couldn't answer. It would be twenty years before I got the answer to my question, but get the answer I did.

In New York during my late-twenties, I got the chance to sail on a friend's 27-foot sloop, where on our first short trip I learned about the principle of lift. Just as an airplane is lifted off the ground by its wings, a boat is pulled through the water because of the shape and position of its sails. The trick, I learned, is to get the right shape in the sail in order to capture the power of the wind.

"So I had it all wrong," I thought. "A boat isn't blown away at all, it's pulled."

To most non-sailors this comes as a big surprise. Rarely does the wind *push* a sailing vessel, and then, only when it blows directly from behind, where it works on only one of the eight points of sail. Most of the time the boat is propelled through the water, the principle of lift acting upon the sails, pulling it forward through the waves, like an aircraft being pulled up, up and away into the wild blue yonder.

When a sailboat is being pushed by the wind, it's called Running with the Wind and it's one of the quietest points of sail. The wind, the boat and the waves are all moving in the same direction and it can feel eerily calm to feel the wind and the boat moving as one. Your chips don't blow off your plate and your hat stays comfortably on your head.

When leaders push, it is seldom the same. Instead of pushing *with* their employees, blowing in the same direction, they tend to push against them, especially when they get resistance or opposition to their vision or direction. That's when leaders flaunt the dreaded "I'm the boss, *that's* why!" excuse and begin demanding rather than persuading.

Can you do that as a captain? Fire up the motor and force your way forward? Sure, but that's not sailing, that's not leading, and that's not taking advantage of the power and talent of your team. Instead, the crew that is pushed simply becomes a group of passengers along for the ride, with no vested interest, commitment or loyalty. And as any seasoned captain will tell you, Loyalty beats Obedience hands down. Loyalty will weather the storms and step up beyond the call of duty, while Obedience jumps ship at the first safe port following a conflict.

True captains, like great leaders, rarely push, and when they do, it's not in opposition to the flow and direction of their people. Instead, they push with them, moving in the same direction. And with a well-led crew, a vessel can absolutely sail towards the wind, across the wind or nearly straight into the wind and make fantastic progress. A boat need not be at the mercy of the forces of nature; it needs simply to harness the power of lift. The same is true in leadership. The more effectively a leader lifts his team up with his vision and direction, the more efficiently they will reach their destination together.

Real leaders don't insist on compliance. Rather, they are committed to lifting their people up. Like filling the sails with wind and power, they give their people shape and purpose. And when the winds of change blow across their surface real leaders sit up and notice, puff out their chest and, quite simply, become a better version of themselves.

HOLDING SPACE

In coaching there is a technique referred to as "holding space" for your client. As a young coach it was a concept that evaded me for years. Coming from a logical, non-emotional upbringing, holding space was a concept I simply couldn't get my brain around. It wasn't that I didn't want to, I just had no context by which I could relate to the process.

I've read that when Columbus approached the New World, the Native Americans didn't even see the boats. It's not that they never looked out into the water. They physically and literally couldn't see them, even though the boats were in plain sight to be seen. They simply had no experience of tall sailing ships; their eyes and their minds couldn't pick them up. That's how they were overcome so easily.

And that's how I was with holding space for my clients. I didn't get it because I had no context for it. Then one day I became aware and I got it, and now I explain it like this:

Sometimes we human beings need to swing our arms wildly and violently and scream crazy thoughts just to see what's there. Then we are done, we put down our arms, tuck in our shirts and move on as if nothing had happened, because what we found there, we didn't want. Or, perhaps we find that we

do want it, we just don't really know until we are free to challenge others' level of comfort with our plan.

Two-year olds do this all the time, and so do adults. Until
we have a chance to go there, we think it's exactly what we
want. We lament and mope and fuss and gripe about not being able to get there. The problem is that in our "real world"
there is no opportunity to go there because when we start
swinging our arms, we hit stuff and people who are too close
to us. We start exploring crazy ideas, just to hear how they
sound. But when people get hit by our swinging arms or hear
our crazy thoughts, they can get freaked-out and either hit
back or try to shape us in their own likeness and image, in
one way or another. They aren't comfortable with our explo-
ration; they want to calm us down or show us the ramifica-
tions of our rants. And sometimes that's not bad, but you still
need and want to go there.

That's where coaching comes in. As a coach, I literally,
emotionally and figuratively "hold space" for the client who
needs to experience this process. She can swing her arms all
she wants. She can say what she needs to say, because I won't
judge her for it. I will simply experience it alongside her and
explore the journey so we can figure out what she meant rather than what she said. This process is one of the most powerful gifts of coaching because there is no other relationship
in our life that observes us without an agenda or opinion.
Nowhere else are we truly free to explore.

Now imagine, just for a moment, the possibility that as a leader of yourself, you gave yourself the permission to go to the crazy, scary, dark, exciting, totally-different-than-anything-else-you've-ever-done-in-your-entire-life places of thoughts and words, all without judgment. What might you give yourself permission to let go of? Might you find the strength and courage you have sought for years, if not forever? How might you feel if given, just for a moment, the freedom to be perfectly who you are?

Now take it one step further. What if a leader – your boss, manager, pastor, friend – could give you that same space? How might your work experience be different, if you were truly free to be you? How might you engage? What possibilities might show up?

People who come to me hating their job and wanting change are suffering from two consistent ills. First, they don't feel respected at work and as a result they aren't free to be themselves and live their dreams. Second, they simply lack the clarity of what they want as an alternative.

When someone espouses a high-level vision and people get excited, what do they ask? They ask, "How are we going to do that?"

"Great! We're going to change the world."

"How?"

What they are really saying is, "I love that idea, I just can't see *how* it's going to be done."

How many times have you listened to a great leader and loved what they said until the details came out and you found yourself thinking, "Oh, that's not what I thought she meant."

I felt that in my previous company as it grew, and I have felt it with various political leaders when the details of their vision didn't match the promise.

Are you holding space to discover *your* vision? Do your details match your promise? Can you spell out precisely how things will look when it is realized? And finally, are you holding space to allow others to fit into the vision you've created?

THE WORD YES

True leaders don't like the word Yes…

At least not in the sense of building a team of Yes People, or creating an environment of clones. An environment of Yes People and clones doesn't cover enough bases. It doesn't bring enough diversity of talent and perspective to be successful long term. Instead, Yes-Sir and Yes-Ma'am engenders a culture for dictators to manage ideas and carry out orders.

True leaders want and need more than that. They recognize that with a powerful team they can create something bigger than themselves. They honestly admit that they themselves don't have all the answers and that they alone can't see all the obstacles or devise all the solutions.

When true leaders seek to build a team, they look to attract people who will be courageous enough to disagree, challenge, question and ponder. Like the captain of a mighty sailing rig, they seek the wind. They seek powerful forces they can harness and use along with economic forces, competition, material costs, all of which influence their vessel constantly. Those opposing forces contain the very power that will fill the sails, convert it to energy, and propel the vision forward.

The question is not, "Do your people agree with you?" The

question is "Can you lead?" Can you create an environment that others want to be a part of? Can you form true connections that tie the team together in deep and meaningful ways, despite differences?

WINNERS AND WINNING

With the likes of Charlie Sheen and his tiger blood, winning has become cliché. Like Charlie, we sometimes have the notion that winning is black and white, us against them. But winning is so much more than the simple annihilation of an opponent, although that seems like the most cherished version of victory in our culture. Winning has a complexity to it, a nuanced integration of both rewards and perceptions. For instance, winning by cheating is seldom respected except by other cheaters observing and not being directly effected by the cheat.

With winning, the eternal question becomes, when I look in the mirror, do I admire the face that looks back? Can I look him in the eye? Can I smile, knowing that I played fair and with the level of integrity that I seek in myself? If the answers are no, than winning isn't winning at all, and few can sustain the celebration of such a hollow victory for long.

When we lay our head on the pillow at night, whose day did we live, our own or someone else's? How much of our win truly belongs to us? And can we argue that a day of loss and defeat is actually a day of winning and success?

I believe that we can. When playing by our own standards,

when living up to our own expectations, when holding true to the integrity we have set for our own lives, we can actually lose the battle and see the day as a win. Conversely, when we win by unfair means, through the abuse of others, by cheating or through manipulation, we find ourselves restless in the night, unsettled and looking back over the day, searching desperately for the "me" in the victory.

Winning isn't always about the highest score or the lowest strokes, the fastest speed or the furthest hit, as some would have us believe. The end does not justify the means by any cost. Others will cheat and yet, if we try to one-up them, all our integrity won't matter a bit because we will be out of work, out of business or out of the playoffs.

There's a great song by Chris de Burgh called *Spanish Train*. It tells the story of the Devil and the Lord gambling for souls, with a refraining line that says, "the Devil still cheats and wins most souls, and as for the Lord, well, he's just doing his best." It's true that others can cheat and beat us, but we can't win by cheating them first. We can't change the game by playing with tainted rules. If we are to change the way business is done, if we are truly going to create an environment that enriches and empowers all, then we must play it differently, drown out the cheaters rather than trying to beat them at their own game.

Winning is a mental game of precision, perseverance and flexibility. These principles hold true whether we are talking about sports, politics, or business. If your head is right, if your focus is clear, if your routine is iron-clad, if your process is tested and proven, you will win more than you lose.

Study the greats, from Andre Agassi to Wayne Gretzky to Jack Welch, and they will all tell you the same thing in their own way: "The *what* doesn't win championships; it is the *why* that wins every time."

Tim Gallwey, who has written many books on the mental game of golf and tennis says, *"There are more players that have the talent to be the best in the world than there are winners."*

Perhaps that's because in any contest there can only be one winner. More likely, however, it's because the head trumps one's talent. Like the cliché story of the elephant being tied to a post at birth, he believes forever more that he can't break free, regardless that his size and power out-match the strength of the rope and post. It's the mental talk we feed ourselves on a monthly, weekly, daily, hourly, momentary basis.

What makes successful, happy people successful and happy is that they get out of their own way more often than the rest of us. Where most of us battle fear, doubt and insecurity on a daily basis and must first defeat those forces before tackling any other foe throughout the day, winners have already won those battles. They wake up ready to take on the next challenge. And don't underestimate the battles of fear, doubt, insecurity and self-sabotage! They have defeated many a warrior before he ever got a chance to wield the sword, much less cut down his enemy with it.

What battle are you fighting? What battle is your team fighting? What battle is each individual on your team fighting? If fear of losing, fear of failure, fear of losing one's job, fear of being wrong, fear of humiliation, embarrassment etc. is the first thing you face, you will not be winners. As a leader, it is your job to recognize such fears and sabotaging talk and to help to eliminate them.

BIG MAN ON CAMPUS

Imagine the following picture.

I'm a recent college graduate. A young twenty-three. At best, I look seventeen, until you put a suit on me. Then I resemble an elementary school kid trying out for a role in the class play dressed up in his older brother's clothes. Nevertheless, I have arrived at the local high school for my first official teaching assignment. As a new substitute teacher, I'm doing my best to look the part while hoping not to be confused with one of the underclassmen.

Truth be told, I walked into that high school experiencing both sheer terror and the lightheaded feeling that occurs moments before passing out cold. In other words, I was in perfect form to be standing before six periods of Home Economics. Probably the worst substitute class assignment ever, this one fell on my first day of teaching.

I arrived early, eager to do a good job and get the hell out as fast I could. I checked in with the office and received a kind welcome. Looking back on it now, I realize that the smiling faces of the secretaries said, "Oh, that poor dear. We will likely never see *him* again, even if he makes it out of there alive."

Nevertheless, I strode confidently to my classroom, unpacked the envelope of instructions and got ready for the day ahead. Slowly my heart calmed down as imagined horrors failed to unfold. In fact, the school was nice, the kids I passed in the halls were friendly, and I marveled at the Home Ec classroom which was clean, well-organized, and had lots of windows.

Do you know the prayer that says, "Dear God, so far it has been a pretty good day. I haven't hurt anyone, my kids still love me and I have been nothing but the perfect husband to my wife. So far I have done a fantastic job at work and no major catastrophes have occurred. But in a few minutes I am going to get out of bed…"

Up until the moment the first students entered the room, I was a pretty darn good sub. Feeling okay, as if I could actually do the job, I stood at the desk sorting papers when a young lady loped into the room and introduced herself.

"Hi! I'm here to give you a fair warning. You may not realize it yet, but in your first period is a guy we call BMOC."

"BMOC?" I asked with a "what-am-I-supposed-to-do-with-this-information" kind of look.

"You know, BMOC. Big Man On Campus. He's big, he's mean and he's the nemesis of every substitute teacher at this school. It's best to just let him do what he wants."

I nodded slowly, desperately trying to think of something mature, wise and intelligent to say in response to this information. About all that came out was, "Are you serious?"

"Oh yes," she said, "I am very serious. He has cornered teachers in the parking lot after school because they challenged him."

Now I don't remember exactly what happened next; the urge to soil my suit surely crossed my mind. But I do remember that I smiled, let out a nervous laugh, and blurted, "Oh, thanks!"

"You're welcome," she said as she turned on her heels and joined her friends tittering in the hall.

Right about then I panicked. I mean, PANICKED! The last thing I'd planned for this day was getting beaten up in the parking lot by a punk who thinks he owns the school. I mean if I'd known *that* was going to happen, I wouldn't have worn dress shoes. I would have worn sneakers in hopes of running faster scared than BMOC could ever run mad. The next ten minutes seemed like hours as I contemplated how to handle the situation. Try though I did, I couldn't come up with ANYTHING that gave me confidence. Just as I thought to go to another teacher to ask for help, the students began to arrive.

Now let me tell you something about this place. It was roomy, with stoves, refrigerators, sinks and cupboards all around the perimeter. In the middle were a couple of large square tables that sat sixteen students each. According to the roster I knew that I had twenty-eight in this first class. What confused me was that the kids all sat at the table on my left, even pulling chairs from the other table to accommodate their numbers. I sat on the edge of my desk, greeting them with "hello" and "how's it going," watching with anxious curiosity, trying desperately to ID BMOC. "If he's in the room," I thought, "he's one hell of a chameleon!"

At last the bell sounded, the door closed, class was expected to begin, and there I stood, leaning against my desk, looking at twenty-five students crammed around one table while the other table sat completely empty.

Sensing my confusion, the young lady who'd given me the warning said, "We save that one for BMOC."

"Oh," I offered, in what I hoped would come across as a casual tone. "Where is he?"

A soft laughter murmured across the table. Shrugging her shoulders the girl said, "Who knows? But he'll be here."

As if on queue, the door opened and in walked three arrogant young men. They confidently strutted to the open table, talking among themselves and nodding an occasional "Whusup?" to the other students, as they settled in, backwards on their chairs. Meanwhile, hand close to her chest, my protector was pointing as discreetly as possible, indicating the fact so obvious that even I, lowly substitute teacher, had figured it out. One of these gentlemen was BMOC, and I was pretty sure I knew which one.

"How nice of you to join us." I said. "Which one of you is BMOC?" At this, the class burst out laughing, with the three fellows laughing as well, until one proudly spoke up.

"My reputation 'proceeds' me."

"Yes, yes it does. Nice to meet you… alrighty, then. Now that the grand entrances are complete, how about we get to know the rest of the class," I said as I commenced taking roll.

To understand what happened next, you need to know that there was only one instruction in my envelope along with the class assignment. The instruction was that no one, under *any* circumstances, was to remove ANY food or drink from the fridge or cupboards.

So when about three minutes into class BMOC stood up and began moving toward the fridge, you can understand why I suddenly found myself in a cold sweat with visions of parking lot violence flashing through my head. Accompanying this unwelcome vision was a painful voice saying "Hey! Tell him to sit down. He's not allowed to eat the food. If they get away with it in your first period, you will have *no* respect from any of the students for the rest of the day, or the rest of your visits to this school, for that matter. *You must stop him!*"

Now let me make it clear. I had no idea *whatsoever* about how to stop BMOC from doing anything he damn well pleased. And I didn't have time to figure it out. All I knew was that I had to act, and fast.

Suddenly it hit me! I *was* the teacher, after all. I held the title. I supposedly had the authority. I just needed to wield my power and everything would be fine. The problem was, it didn't feel fine. I didn't feel either powerful or authoritative and my "position" didn't seem to offer me any value whatsoever. In that moment the only question rolling around in my head was "How?" How was I going to solve this problem?

"Hey, BMOC. What's up?" I ventured.

"I'm getting' a drink, man. You got a prob'em with that?"

"Uh, well, as a matter of fact, I do. Please take a seat."

"I will, man. As soon as I get a drink."

"Uh, no. Without the drink." I said, taking a big, dry swallow. "Please take a seat."

"Who the hell do you think you're talkin' to? Do you know who I am?"

"Well, you keep responding to 'BMOC' and 'Big Man' so I would have to assume that, yes, I know who I am talking with."

I said this trying desperately to strike a tone between confidence, respect and matter-of-factness. I prayed that no one could see my knees shaking like leaves in a hurricane.

"Come on, man, please sit down. No one is to take any food or drink from the kitchen," I reasoned. "So I'm asking you nicely to return to your seat."

At this point the room was dead silent. Poor BMOC was in a very awkward position, and his two buddies were in rapt attention. His peers were expecting cool, I was expecting compliance, and he was protecting a reputation. For some reason the Kenny Rodgers' song *The Gambler* began rolling through my head.

"…You've got to…
Know when to hold 'em,
Know when to fold 'em,
Know when to walk away,
And know when to run…"

Man, did I want to run. At the very least, I thought I should fold, let him do what he wanted and simply report the incident to the office at the end of the day. But I didn't. I held 'em. I just sat casually on the edge of the desk with my hands next to me rather than crossed in defiance, and I watched. I didn't know what else to say, so I didn't say anything. I just watched, doing my best not to lock into a staring contest with BMOC, but rather, to just observe, hoping the next step would reveal itself to me.

"You know I own this school, right?"

"I've been told."

"I can do what I want."

He had a point. It's not like I could *make* him do anything. For a moment my dad's line ran through my head: "You're right, I can't 'make' you, but I can make you wish you *would* have!" That's when it dawned on me that I had absolutely no idea how to make him wish he'd have listened to me. So I simply said,

"Then I'm asking you to *want* to sit down without a drink. I am asking you to *want* to play by the rules of the school *you* own. And I'm asking, please sit down."

"What are you going to do if I don't?" asked BMOC.

I looked him square in the eye and called his bluff with one of my own.

"That's a great question. I don't know. If you insist on getting a drink, then we will both find out."

That's the moment we truly saw one another. BMOC looked deep into my eyes. I have no idea what he saw, but he bit his lower lip, mumbled something under his breath, and headed back to his seat. His last comment for the rest of the period was simply, "This ain't over, man!"

I smiled a crooked smile, shrugged my shoulders and moved on with the class assignment. As the students worked, I sat wondering how I would make it to my car without getting ambushed.

When class was over, everyone dutifully waited for BMOC and his entourage to exit. As they did, BMOC pointed to me and said, "Watch your back, man!" The rest of the class filed out, some congratulating me, others warning me. The young lady who'd first warned me said, "Wow, I've never seen him do that before."

Later that day I headed to my car feeling pretty good about myself. BMOC's threat had long faded. No other class had been remotely as challenging as first period, an experience that seemed like ancient history by the end of my long day. I was simply exhausted and ready to go home. But as I turned the last corner to my car, BMOC came up behind me.

"How was the rest of our day little man?"

I smiled uncontrollably. Little man. Funny. That's what my grandmother used to call me.

"It was good, actually. After you, the day got infinitely easier. How was yours, Big Man?"

"You're a weird dude, man."

And then there was a long but not wholly awkward pause.

"For such a small guy, you've got balls."

He leaned back. I tensed up, then relaxed and reached out my hand. To my surprise, he shook it and said, "See you next time, man."

And he did. I was called back a few days later to sub for the second worst class, Physical Education. Third period, just before lunch, guess who walked through the door? You got it. BMOC. He saw me, lit up, greeted me as "Mr. F" and we were friends forever after. If I needed help controlling a class, BMOC took the lead. I received nothing but respect from the students in that school because BMOC thought I was weird, but cool.

CONCLUSION

Leadership is less about power and more about people. It's less about authority and more about connection. Leadership often places us in a position where we don't feel worthy because we don't know it all, because others seem to be more influential than we are, or because we feel like we're in over our head. Yet leadership really isn't about having all the answers, or never making mistakes. It's about the courage to be who we are while respecting others for who they are.

Big Man On Campus might have perceived my actions as aggressive or threatening, but he didn't. That's because I treated him with respect. I allowed him to hold onto his title, position, and reputation, without mocking or disrespecting him. I neither pulled rank nor put him down. By asking him to honor the rules of the school he "owned," I offered him an out that allowed us each to get what we wanted. More than that, by acknowledging his own self-respect, I enabled BMOC to grow into the student who valued and respected others in return. His once destructive pride of ownership could be channeled in ways that improved the very institution with which he identified.

In the end, people don't respect you because they agree with you. They respect you because they admire your conviction and your clarity. They feel your authenticity and understand at a core level when you are being honest, and genuine, rather than manipulative.

In this case, as in many others, First Dimensional Leadership – merely wielding authority – would not have worked. It was only by stepping up to the Second Dimension, being genuinely myself, that I invited BMOC to engage his own Second Dimensional Leadership. And when one is fully engaged in leadership of self, that's when the Third Dimension kicks in. BMOC *willingly* followed precisely because of the genuine connection we made that fateful day in first period Home Economics.

For me, what makes a great leader great is the ability to truly and deeply see people; to see their worth, their potential, their beauty, their strength and to open up a space that allows all the potential greatness to emerge. It's not a battle but a partnership. And it's a partnership that we owe to ourselves as much as we owe it to others that we lead. And yet, leading ourselves with such compassion, such esteem, such openness and forgiveness can be the hardest form of leadership of all.

As the eastern mystics have taught us: "*An eye cannot see itself, a tooth cannot bite itself, a knife cannot cut itself.*" Not seeing our own worthiness as clearly as we see the worthiness of another is exactly like the eye that cannot see itself. It's not that we alone are not worthy. It's that we are blinded by self-judgment, distracted by our own insider information. Looking outside ourselves at others we do not have the same access to their hidden feelings, or secret failures. And that is the gift true leaders long to share, the ability to drop judgments about others to just enjoy the pure experience of them. That's why we *all* need real and powerful leaders in our lives to help us see what we can not see, to believe what we may struggle to believe, to step up to a level of perfection within us that is so powerful that it only takes someone holding up the mirror. When we can convert judgments into insights, we embellish our vision, connect meaningfully to others, and create a story worth living.

It is this powerful aspect of leadership – the ability to truly see in others what they cannot, do not, see in themselves – that engages the team. Just like the sail taking the power of the wind and converting it into a graceful energy that propels the vessel forward, leaders – you and I – also have the potential to move ourselves and others to the uncharted waters of our dreams and visions.

APPENDIX I
QUESTIONS A LEADER ASKS

When you say you want to be a great leader, what do you mean? One way to find out is by asking yourself the following powerful questions.

- Who is my role model?
- What does being a great leader look like?
- "Great," by what standard?
- "Leader," by what definition?
- If I could observe myself being the great leader I seek to be, what would I see?
- What is observable in those following me to make it crystal clear that they follow a great leader?
- What kind of culture will I create?
- How will I respond to disagreement?
- How will I respond to insubordination?
- What will I dress like?
- What car will I drive?
- How will I define my income in relationship to my employees?
- How will my employees feel about their level of income in comparison to mine?
- What happens when as a successful leader I begin to

think my success is all about me?

These questions beg other important questions. As a great leader, do you care what your followers think? Do you see your followers simply as team members, as expendable, or something more? Do you create jobs or careers? What kind of impact do you want to have on the world?

As you can see, this is a formidable list and it goes on, the more your leadership grows.

Most people who come to me to become better leaders aren't bad leaders. They just lack the level of detail necessary to answer the questions they are facing along the way. And because we aren't really taught to think with this level of detail, we have a tendency to go to someone else for the answers. We are taught that if you need to know something, ask an expert. The problem is that there is only one expert regarding what kind of leader – person, mother, contributor, etc. – you want to be. That's you!

APPENDIX II
THE VALUES TIMELINE

The Values Timeline looks like this:

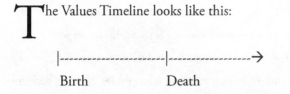

The first vertical line represents the day you were born. The second vertical line represents the moment of your death. The space between your death and the vertical line furthest to the right is, can you guess it? That's right, your legacy! Whether you are conscious of it or not, believe in it or not, you *will* have a legacy. What kind of legacy depends completely on what happens between the time of your birth and your death.

Of course no one knows for certain when they will die. The purpose of this exercise isn't to debate the merits of thinking about death. In no way am I planning to hold you to this secondary number. It is simply a marker for the purposes of the exercise. Indeed, when describing the guidelines for this exercise, I often hear crazy comments and jokes until I go on to explain that while we may not know our exact age at death, most of us have a fairly specific perception of how long we will live based on any number of factors, from when our parents died, our life-style, actuary tables…there are even websites that can help you predict how long you will live. When examined, we all have an idea of about how long we expect to live.

Now, somewhere between 0, i.e. birth, and the age of your death, is your current age. Draw a line between 0 and death that then represents your current age. So if you expect to live to 100 and you are 50, draw a vertical line centered halfway between 0 and 100. You can immediately see that everything to the left of your current age represents the past, your history, the part of your story already written. Everything between your current age and death is unwritten history, sometimes called the future.

Between birth and your current age is all the life you have lived. Some of it was fantastic, some of it sad, happy, boring, scary, miraculous and disastrous. Much of it you probably could recall if you wanted, while other parts of it you couldn't forget for love or money. That's the part we want to focus on, the stuff you can't forget.

So, on the timeline between 0 and now, place a tick for each of the unforgettable events, at approximately the age that it occurred. Some of these events will have been great successes, others great failures, and still other purely mundane, but for some reason they stick in your mind, even though they may seem to have no obvious significance. Whatever they are, simply drop the judgment and note the event with a word or two.

Once you have captured all the events of significance – and please take the time to be exhaustive – go back through them and next to each one write down which values of yours were honored or dishonored during that event.

Let's take a sporting event, for example, which might honor your value of fair play, or competition, or winning. Other events might expose your value of laughter, or tears. (Yes, some people, as they explore this process, realize they enjoy a really good cry every so often.)

As you jot down the values represented by the series of events in your life, what you are *not* looking for are the high-level values you learned in Sunday school. You know, things like honesty, love and respect, to name a few. It's not that they're unimportant, it's that they are generally so high-level that they are rarely lived in our daily practice of life. When it comes to every day living, that is, our core decision-making criteria, we tend to gravitate towards more specific types of values, and those high-level values just aren't specific enough to inform us.

So as you start to reveal your values, think specifically. To help you do that, every time you write a value next to an event, ask yourself what it is about that value that you value. For instance, if you see that the value of money shows up in the form of your first job, and then again when you get a college scholarship, ask what it is *about* money that you value. The value of money may be power, authority or influence, for example. For some, money may represent security. Others drill down into money and see that it represents independence, freedom, or even greed, as I have seen in rare circumstances. For still others, money shows up because they prize winning; it's the competition and the conquest that really drives them.

What does it mean for you? As we ask questions about the significant events of our lives, we are invited to dig down two, three, five levels or more, to drill down into crystal clear and specific truths about our real values. We begin to realize that what we esteem are not the high-level ideas of how one is supposed to be. Instead they are the raw, authentic, and driving forces of who we actually are. Sometimes, we don't even like what they reveal. We may see greed or selfishness, for example, show up as the habitual failure to recognize, evaluate and understand the action we are taking.

In the end, what the exercise shows us is that our values are those things we esteem, the things that have worth for us, the places where we find significance and importance. Put simply, why is one person willing to spend $80,000 on a BMW when another sees the expenditure as an extravagant waste of money? The first individual gets value, worth, reward, pleasure and meaning from the purchase, where the latter gets only an empty wallet. For him, an $80,000 car brings no more reward, pleasure or meaning than a $20,000 car, but make it a hybrid, or a plug-in electric and he'll pay a $10,000 premium for the same vehicle he could otherwise get cheaper. That's where he sees and experiences worth, meaning, pleasure, significance, and reward.

At this point you might be thinking, "Hey, wait a minute, this isn't leadership, it's therapy!" And from one perspective, you might be right. But from another perspective, it isn't therapy either – it's connection! Remember that the secret of effective and powerful leadership lives in the ability to meet people where they are, rather than where we wish they were. By facilitating such an exercise yourself, or by bringing people like me into your organization to facilitate such an exercise with teams, you begin to understand each individual's language; their values and motivations; how they will consciously or unconsciously judge and evaluate you and filter their experiences of their work with you. Understanding this is pure power! And with such an understanding, you can form bonds and create solutions that truly meet the needs of your team.

Imagine, as you lead yourself through the timeline of your life and dreams, what would be possible if you truly understood what you value. What if you could begin to see the patterns in your life? What might you achieve if you were crystal clear about where you truly place significance and meaning in your life? How much better might you lead yourself? What kind of leader would that allow you to be of others? What if you could understand the values of others and provide a forum in which they could begin to find value for themselves?

ABOUT THE AUTHOR

Steven Fulmer is a HUMAN Strategist,™ Inspirational Speaker, Leadership Coach and Author. He is the creator of LifeQuest Mapping™ and The 10-Point Leadership Triangle.™ Steven has inspired thousands with his powerful message of personal leadership. He has not only helped many believe that anything is possible, he has also provided the strategies, tools and path to make it true. Born and raised in Baltimore, Maryland, Steven makes his home in Oregon with his wife and two daughters.

Leadership Just Got Personal

Steven Fulmer
HUMAN Strategist™ | Speaker |
Coach | Author

Steven Fulmer is a successful entrepreneur and Human Strategist™ who started his first business at the age of 16. By 35 he was Vice President of an 85 person, $10 million software company which he was instrumental in growing from three people and $300,000 per year.

Today Steven is a national speaker inspiring Fortune 500 companies, non-profits, associations and emerging leaders. His coaching practice reaches as far away as Australia, and he currently facilitates the personal Mission & Vision Workshop for the internationally recognized
George Fox University MBA Program.

Steven has appeared more than a dozen times on AM Northwest, Portland's premier morning show, and is the co-author of "Speaking of Success" alongside such notable thinkers as Stephen Covey, Ken Blanchard and Jack Canfield.

For bookings and more Information about tailoring Steven's powerful content for your event, company or team, please contact us at:

503.806.0527

Steven@StevenFulmer.com
www.FulmerSpeaks.com
PO Box 91284 | Portland, OR | 97291

CPSIA information can be obtained
at www.ICGtesting.com
Printed in the USA
FSHW021553301019